PENGUIN BOOKS

# Coast to Coast

Kevyn Male was born and bred a country boy, and for the first 15 years of his life, he experienced life in the confines of two country stores his parents Jock and Daize owned and operated. It was this early experience that in part led him to open his own store (3 Bears) on Broadway, Newmarket, in 1966 and 34 years later he still retails (Route 66) from the same location.

He was once described by *Marketing* magazine as an extrovert, an individualist with a boisterous style, and an avowed opponent of petty bureaucracy.

Rugby has always been a passion and he entered the senior ranks in 1961 as an 18-year-old member of the Otahuhu Club. He counts himself privileged to have played alongside the likes of Waka Nathan and Mac Herewini, and was an Auckland rugby representative from 1962–72.

Kevyn has been a prolific author over the years. *Coast to Coast* is his third book with Penguin.

# Coast to Coast

## THE GRASS-ROOTS OF NEW ZEALAND RUGBY

Kevyn Male

PENGUIN BOOKS

# Acknowledgements

The author would like to thank Kath McLean, Bremner Mill, Winston Nepia, John Hill and the team (*Gisborne Herald*) and Tania Takarangi from the East Coast, and John Hunt, Tony Ferguson, Ron Messenger and Doug Sail from Buller and the West Coast.

For their superb contributions in back-up photography, special thanks to Jill Carlyle and Mark Ryan. Thanks also to Tony Ferguson, who has had a long photographic association with the *Westport News*, and to his mate down the road, Doug Sail, the sports editor for the *Greymouth Evening Star*. Finally, thanks to the late Garth Tapper for the illustrations.

PENGUIN BOOKS

Penguin Books (NZ) Ltd, Cnr Rosedale and Airborne Roads, Albany, Auckland 1310, New Zealand
Penguin Books Ltd, 27 Wrights Lane, London W8 5TZ, England
Penguin USA, 375 Hudson Street, New York, NY 10014, United States
Penguin Books Australia Ltd, 487 Maroondah Highway, Ringwood, Australia 3134
Penguin Books Canada Ltd, 10 Alcorn Avenue, Toronto, Ontario, Canada M4V 3B2
Penguin Books India (P) Ltd, 11, Community Centre, Panchsheel Park, New Delhi 110017, India
Penguin Books (South Africa) Pty Ltd, 5 Watkins Street, Denver Ext 4, 2094, South Africa

Penguin Books Ltd, Registered Offices: Harmondsworth, Middlesex, England

First published by Penguin Books (NZ) Ltd, 2000

Copyright © Kevyn Male, 2000

Front cover photographs: Top, Ngati Porou polytech students, from left,
James, Hone and Shaun. Bottom, the 1999 West Coast reps fan club.
Back cover photograph: Victor Takarangi with his grandson Karauria Keelan (left)
and friend Hira-John Wharepapa. Insert: a loyal West Coast fan.

1 3 5 7 9 10 8 6 4 2

Typeset by Amy Tansell at Egan-Reid Ltd, Auckland
Printed in Hong Kong by Toppan Printing

ISBN 0 14 029874 6

# Contents

The turned up collar looks more threatening mate.!! Gav lds

# Introduction

GROWING UP AND attending school in a rural area had certain limitations, and being party to an organised game of rugby was one of them.

Half-inflated fat leather balls, tea-tree sticks for goal posts and a makeshift field in the neighbour's cow paddock were more or less the order of the day. As a five-year-old, I envied kids who owned a pair of boots – I copped my first prized pair for my tenth birthday!

When I first entered the ranks of the Otahuhu seniors as an 18-year-old, all of a sudden playing the game of rugby took on a whole new meaning. Two years further down the track, I had my first taste of how it felt to pull on the blue-and-white hoops for Auckland during a game at Ruatoria – Auckland Colts v. East Coast.

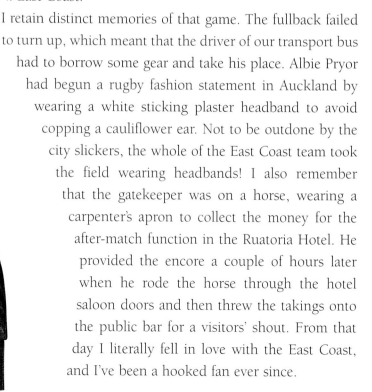

I retain distinct memories of that game. The fullback failed to turn up, which meant that the driver of our transport bus had to borrow some gear and take his place. Albie Pryor had begun a rugby fashion statement in Auckland by wearing a white sticking plaster headband to avoid copping a cauliflower ear. Not to be outdone by the city slickers, the whole of the East Coast team took the field wearing headbands! I also remember that the gatekeeper was on a horse, wearing a carpenter's apron to collect the money for the after-match function in the Ruatoria Hotel. He provided the encore a couple of hours later when he rode the horse through the hotel saloon doors and then threw the takings onto the public bar for a visitors' shout. From that day I literally fell in love with the East Coast, and I've been a hooked fan ever since.

A couple of seasons later I cracked a similar experience with the Auckland As during a match against the West Coast. In typical Coast fashion, no stone was left unturned in the hospitality stakes. The 'Dirt Trackers' (reserves) sat on a makeshift grandstand on the back of a raised truck tray parked right on halfway.

The warmth of the people who live on the Coast was further endorsed that night by the music of the famed Kokatahi Band and a sumptuous post-match seafood spread.

The spark that prompted me to write this book came as a result of what I consider to be one of the greatest games of rugby ever played in New Zealand. East Coast clinched the 1999 NPC Third Division title by defeating their neighbours from Poverty Bay to the tune of 18–15, and such was the spirit of the match and the atmosphere at the ground, that it's a pity one team had to leave the field without the title.

I'm honoured to have met some wonderful New Zealanders while compiling this book. The camaraderie, the humour and the hospitality of rural New Zealand only further confirms my long-held theory that rural rugby clubs are the main focal points of small communities – and the grass-roots of the game in New Zealand.

Kevyn Male
*October 2000*

East Coast

# Foreword

AS ONE OF twenty-seven affiliates of the NZRFU, East Coast is recognised demographically as the smallest provincial union in New Zealand with a population base of 6500–7000 (90% Ngati Porou). Sport in general, but rugby in particular, is the catalyst that unites all our communities. Through kohanga reo, clubs, sub-unions and marae, rugby is an integral part of the whanau (family) life. The golden years of the 1950s and 60s saw a number of All Blacks and Maori All Blacks selected from the East Coast.

The issue of amalgamation has been on the national agenda for thirty years. This has served to remind our administrators of the importance of rugby to our people and is no longer an issue for us.

The success of 1999, winning the 3rd Division NPC final, was a fairy-tale ending to the century.

In 1997 we celebrated 75 years as a union and the first-ever visit of a NZRU Chairman, Rob Fisher. We are determined to celebrate one hundred years of East Coast Rugby in 2022.

Bill Burdett
*Chairman East Coast RFU*

# A proud tradition

SIZE DOESN'T MATTER when it comes to greatness. Some of our finest moments in rugby have come from our smallest unions. And so it is with the East Coast Union. It was founded in 1921 and during the decade that followed there were few better periods that epitomised the strength and magnificence of New Zealand Maori rugby. Jimmy Mill, one of the great All Black half-backs of his day, and the immortal George Nepia were the pride and joy of East Coast and All Black rugby during this era.

The late 1950s and early 60s are often described as the 'Golden Era' of East Coast rugby. In 1958, East Coast won seven of their nine representative fixtures, including the prized scalps of Poverty Bay and Hawke's Bay. The coast produced some wonderful rugby talent then. Such names as Karaka, Reedy, Moeke, Henare, Watson and Kururangi filled every household and pub then. The union hit the jackpot in 1958 when one of the great men of NZ Maori rugby, Eddie Whatarau, came to town and took up a two-year teaching position in Ruatoria.

And as well as the illustrious George Nepia and Jimmy Mill, the union lays claim to having bred and nurtured three further All Blacks – Buff Milner (1970), Andy Jefferd (1980) and Robert Kururangi (1978) – although Milner and

Kururangi were selected while playing for other teams.

The East Coasters are proud, staunch people for whom rugby beats strongly in the heart of their community. Is it any surprise then that this, the smallest union in the country, should snatch the coveted NPC Third Division title in 1999.

Credit for the deed goes not only to the players but also the likes of coach

Joe McClutchie – doubly rewarded that year with the title of New Zealand's Coach of the Year – and current union chairman, Bill Burdett. There would be few better grass-roots rugby administrators than this man. In acknowledging that New Zealand's smallest union won the third division title, he also points out that the marvellous result was achieved at no small cost.

Small unions like the East Coast, West Coast and Buller Unions rely almost entirely on outside sponsorship to compete, and the cost of maintaining an annual representative programme on the East Coast is in the vicinity of $100,000. With these small rural unions, sponsorship dollars via local industry is almost negligible. Instead companies like Air New Zealand and the brewery giants Lion and DB must provide the sponsorship dollars. In so doing, they provide a lifeline for all of those involved in the game at rural level.

If our national rugby is to flourish and once more dominate the international arena, then it is absolutely essential that club rugby standards and growth be maintained in the grass-roots regions of rural New Zealand.

# Hall of fame

## George Nepia

Born in 1905 in Wairoa, George Nepia was one of the great Titans of international rugby. He represented New Zealand from 1924 to 1930, and played 46 matches for the All Blacks. He reached the pinnacle of his career during the famous Invincibles tour of Great Britain (1924–25) where he took the field in all of the 30 matches played.

Between 1935–37 he switched codes to play rugby league in England, but returned to rugby when he came back to New Zealand, appearing twice more for East Coast at the age of 42. Aged 45, George played his last first-class game against Poverty Bay in a team that was captained by his son George junior, who later died on active service in 1954 while serving with the army in Malaya.

George died in Ruatoria in 1986 at the age of 81. Even today his grave at Waiapu is a mecca for those who want to commemorate one of the great legends of the game.

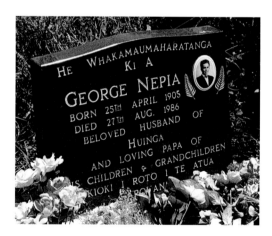

**ABOVE**: George Nepia's grave at Waiapu has become a local mecca for rugby enthusiasts.

**LEFT**: Nepia was 19 when he first gained selection as an All Black (1924–25).

# Morning tea with the Nepias

Of George Nepia's four children, two are still living in the Ruatoria region – George's youngest son Winston and his only daughter, Kiwi. During a recent trip to the East Coast I was invited by Winston to morning tea at Kiwi's home.

This region is spiritually significant to Maori. Mt Hikurangi looms in the background, and the constant sea-spray and mist enveloping the area adds to the mystery. Current pride of place now goes to a waka dominating a coastal paddock near the mouth of the Rangitukia River while it awaits crucial sea trials.

Listening to Winston and Kiwi talk about the early days with their dad only confirmed the opinion that George Nepia had the same mana on the playing field as he did off it. Waiapu is the final resting place of New Zealand's favourite rugby son, George Nepia. Morning tea with this most special family is an experience to be cherished, and Kiwi's Christmas cake was pretty special as well!

ABOVE: Winston and Kiwi Nepia.

BELOW: The waka awaiting sea trials at the Rangitukia River mouth near Tikitiki after being shifted from its construction site at Whangara.

## Henare (Buff) Milner

Buff Milner gained All Black honours as a member of Ivan Vodanovich's team to South Africa in 1970. He was born in Tokomaru Bay in 1946, and began playing representative rugby with the East Coast in 1963.

Buff had a first-class career of 157 games over 16 seasons, and I had the pleasure of touring with him as a member of the 1964 Colts team to Australia.

## Kath McLean

For the past 23 years Kath McLean has been in many ways the patron saint of the East Coast Union.

During that time she has been a tireless worker not only for the union but also in all aspects of daily life within the community. She has been East Coast's secretary/treasurer since 1975, and has attended all NZRFU annual meetings for the past 24 years.

Be it attending to the needs of junior grade rugby, taking her turn in the Ruatoria main ground ticket box on rep day, or helping individuals and families in need, this very 'special' lady has always been there.

# Victor (VJ) Takarangi

Victor Takarangi started his rugby career with the East Coast Union in 1966 at the age of 21 and played his last game in 1984 at the age of 39. In all he played 108 games for the union.

Yet perhaps his most famous moment came as a spectator. The East Coast Rugby Union in conjunction with David Batty from Gisborne was running a 'Kick for Cash' competition that was held at every home game of the East Coast team.

Supporters had to purchase a programme at the gate and just before half-time two programme numbers were drawn. The lucky programme holder was given the opportunity to 'Kick for Cash'. As no one had been successful in previous weeks, the stakes were raised from $10,000 to $20,000. The kick had to be taken before the second half resumed.

On 4 October 1998, Victor finally got his chance when his number came up. He pulled his trusty boots and black and white Hikurangi club socks from the boot of the car and walked out onto the field. As he prepared to kick, the crowd grew silent for they knew if anyone could get the kick VJ could.

The kick was from 45 metres in front of the posts. He lined his ball up, eyed the goal and stepped back. He took two deep breaths and then ran forward and kicked the ball for all it was worth in toe hack fashion. Away the ball flew through the air – with hundreds of pairs of eyes on it. It went to the right, wobbled, straightened and then sailed victoriously through the goal posts. Horns tooted, people yelled and screamed congratulations, and dozens ran on the field to shake his hand.

**Great stuff Vic – KM**

# Club scene

LIKE MOST RUGBY unions in New Zealand, the East Coast has few problems with the growth of the game at junior and teenage level. Over the last few years the number of juniors playing Saturday morning rugby has swollen to nearly 700 players – largely in response to the local union's development programme and its emphasis on fun and skill development.

The senior club level, however, is a little different. Long travelling distances and limited work opportunities have unfortunately whittled away the numbers, but winning the NPC Third Division title should put a little more fire in the bellies of those wanting some action from the club scene.

East Coasters give it 'heaps' during the game and it's no secret that they give it plenty more long after the match is over. The players and supporters possess a rugby culture that is unique to the East Coast, and it would be a rash act if anyone in the NZRU hierarchy made any attempt to change it.

ABOVE: Anthony Nelson (left) and Jimmy Aupouri (right) – the driving force behind the local union's development programme.

RIGHT: Bill Burdett, chairman of the East Coast Rugby Union and one of New Zealand's leading rugby administrators.

BELOW: The public bar of the Ruatoria Hotel, and the nerve centre of East Coast rugby – always was and always will be!

# The way we were

Some things never change and on the East Coast rugby has always played an important part of the local culture. Long-time Tokomaru Bay resident and photographer Jill Carlyle took these winter East Coast shots some 20 years ago in the early 1980s. They capture the essence of rugby culture – pride in the local team, lots of support, and a ton of fun.

**ABOVE**: Saving mum the job by washing up at the local swimming pool.

**ABOVE RIGHT**: Post-match wash-up at Hiruharama School, 1982.

**RIGHT**: Junior rugby at its grass-roots best – in the mud, bare footed, and sheer enjoyment.

No prizes for guessing who's winning — Tokomaru Bay United v. Waima, *c.* 1982.

This time the worried expressions betray a different story. The local support crew during a Tokomaru Bay United v. Waima match.

ABOVE: George and Mildred's Tolaga Bay supermarket – proud sponsors and supporters of the Uawa Seniors.

RIGHT: All smiles from Wyntah, Matu and Roland of Tolaga Bay School.

**Anything goes in East Coast rugby including sandshoes, coloured shorts, and socks around the ankles.**

RIGHT: Ruatoria College principal Randolph Te Mara experienced a colourful spell with the East Coast reps during the 1980s and 90s. He started duties as a 90kg half-back and ended his playing days as a 114kg prop.

# The 'little fellas'

ABOVE: Any excuse to get out of school – the 'little fellas' at Tokomaru Bay School. Star of the show is three-year-old Veronica holding the ball.

ABOVE RIGHT: 'Our uncle was an All Black, and he was Andy Jefferd.' Five-year-old Kate and big brother Tim posing in front of their home goal posts at Tolaga Bay.

LEFT: What life is all about – a few mates, an open field, and a rugby ball.

RIGHT: Three up-and-comers from the Hiruharama Marae settlement – four-year-old Tukimihia Gibb, six-year-old Ihaka Gibb, and eight-year-old Paora Wharepapa. When asked whether he would one day like to become an All Black, Ihaka replied, 'Nah, I just want to play for the East Coast.' Shortly after this photo was taken, they called in the tractor and mower to give the field a pre-season mow.

LEFT: Aspiring rugby players on the field of the picturesque bush-clad Te Puia School.

BELOW: The Hiruharama Marae rugby field is a favourite haunt for local kids and their horses.

RIGHT: Victor Takarangi with his grandson Karauria Keelan (left) and friend Hira-John Wharepapa checking out the Hiruharama Marae rugby field prior to its annual mow.

# Feeding the troops

WIN OR LOSE, the average rugby team heads down the road after a match to sit down for a good feed and a few beers. And if your luck's in, and you've been party to a pilgrimage to the East Coast, it's more than likely that sometime during the weekend, you will cop the business end of a post-match hangi or customary boil-up.

And if the Ruatoria Hotel is your bed for the night, and your stomach craves for a late-night feed, then there's the famous Kai Kart across the road. It's a favourite haunt of the locals, and for the past 21 years Mary Mataira has been the one behind the till dishing out the tucker.

Pit-stop kai sign – Te Puia.

Where to go for late–night tucker in Ruatoria – Mary Mataira's famous Kai Kart.

RIGHT: 'Toko' fisherman Sam Waititi who specialises in catching crays, is a staunch supporter of the Uawa Rugby Club.

LEFT: The boil-up is very much par for the course with any post-match feed for a rep fixture on the East Coast – into it goes all manner of seafood, from pipis and mussels to crayfish.

## Two recipes for paparoa takakau (Maori bread)

**1.**

2 cups flour
Water or milk
Pinch of salt
Baking powder optional

- Mix to a sticky consistency and shape with as little handling as possible into a 20 x 10 cm shape.
- Either wrap in tinfoil and throw into fire embers or place in a tin and bake. The burnt crust can be removed before eating. Best served with butter and eaten while hot.

**2.**

4 cups flour
1 teaspoon salt
4 tablespoons baking powder
Milk

- Sieve all ingredients and mix to a soft dough with milk. Turn onto a floured surface and knead lightly into a ball of dough. Press out into a 25–30cm diameter round. Cut through centre both ways into four pieces. Bake in a hot oven for 15–20 minutes.

# The hangi business

## Oven hangi

The meal must be prepared in a roasting dish with a fitting lid. Sprinkle some parsley and a few pieces of diced celery into the dish. Place a few pork bones in the bottom of the dish and then add four pork chops (chicken can be added or used in place of pork chops). Next add four pieces of pumpkin, four potatoes, enough cabbage for four people, and if possible some watercress. Add 1½ cups of water. No salt is needed. Cover the dish and bake for 3½ hours in a moderately hot oven. Serves four.

## Hangi preparation

- Try and obtain volcanic rocks or stones.
- Dig a hole or trench to fit the size of the hangi food baskets.
- Use brushwood manuka and plenty of newspaper and kindling.
- Place the smaller wood near the base of the hole and the brushwood on top.
- Place the stones on top of the brushwood.
- Keep the stone heap burning for 2–3 hours or until they are extremely hot.
- Using shovels, remove the stones and unburnt wood. Clear most of the embers from the hole. Place the stones back into the hole with the food baskets on top.
- Cover with wet sheets, then wet sacking and then more wet sacking or bags on top.
- Cover with loose soil.
- Lift within 2½–3 hours.

**'Easy, eh?'**  Winston Nepia

Preparing the pit – the hangi on the Pakirikiri Marae after a Tologa v. Tokomaru Bay match, 1984.

Most New Zealanders at some stage of their lives have enjoyed the festivities and food associated with a good old-fashioned Maori hangi. An East Coast hangi is more often part of the deal for funerals, birthdays, weddings and notable rugby fixtures. A hangi is only as good as the man in charge, and in this one it's Michael Heeney (in the striped jersey). And with Mt Hikurangi (below) piercing the clouds in the background, it turned out to be a real beauty.

# Fixtures and fittings

WHEN PLAYING THE game most East Coasters stick to the rules, even if most playing fields lack the refinements found in the big city – a point that is often clearly reflected with their tools of trade, the fixtures and the fittings that go with them.

Out here you'll be lucky to find a 10-metre line let alone a corner flag. It's not uncommon for a back-country field to be cleared of grazing stock prior to a game, and getting behind the ute or shed to change into playing gear is executed with little fuss.

Players and supporters alike are notoriously proud of their long-held traditions. East Coasters play a hard bruising game, and local supporters get right behind their players, reliving each game in the post-match festivities that follow.

RIGHT: There was no prouder moment for East Coast rugby than winning the 1999 NPC Third Division title, and largely responsible for the final result – 1999 NPC Coach of the Year, Joe McClutchie.

## East Coast supporters are staunch to the core.

**ABOVE LEFT**: Long-time supporter Dave Waru and his horse Blue doing the morning rounds in Tologa Bay.

**ABOVE RIGHT**: St John Ambulance duty officers and 'Zambuck' supremos on a big-match day at rugby headquarters in Ruatoria – Frances Manuel and Lewis Domb. Their St John duties span from Tokomaru Bay to Cape Runaway.

**LEFT**: Outside the Ruatoria Hotel, Ruatoria, from left, East Coast rugby diehards Terry Collier, Bremner Mill and Jum Reedy.

**ABOVE LEFT**: Long-time East Coast identity Jack Cahill, now retired, on the coast at 'Toko' following a long innings at nearby Ihungia Station.

**ABOVE RIGHT**: A special East Coast fixture – 1999 New Zealand rugby coach of the Year, Joe McClutchie.

**RIGHT**: Boydie Kiri Kiri, the local Anglican minister, and his wife Keri on the doorstep of their home in Tologa Bay.

ABOVE: Faces of the future. James, Hone and Shaun are Ngati Porou polytech students from Ruatoria specialising in ground base cable logging.

LEFT: Kumeroa Smith, the skipper's mum – her son Wirihana Raihania captained the East Coast team to victory in the 1999 NPC Third Division final. Like all rugby mums, she is her son's proudest supporter.

By his own admission Doug Katae
(right) never reached notable
heights as a rugby player during
his playing days 40 years ago. His
regional Matakaoa sub union (Te
Araroa) in the 1960s supported four
major East Coast club teams –
City, Hicks Bay, Wanderers and
Tokararangi – and he still remains
among their most ardent
supporters.

Yet Doug did later achieve fame of
a different type. It was his honour,
while leading a team of 22 bullocks,
to raise the flag at East Cape at the
dawn of the new millennium – an
event witnessed by millions of
viewers worldwide.

LEFT: John Love and his
nephew Robert Love
manage the Maori Land
Corporation station which
forms the boundary
between East Coast and
Poverty Bay rugby.

BELOW: A local business supporting its local hero – the Kiwi Tearooms at Ruatoria doing the honours by sponsoring the East Coast's promising fullback, Doone Harrison.

Ngati Porou — a proud tribal tradition. For many people, Ngati Porou is the East Coast.

One of the most active promoters of local rugby and Maori culture on the Coast is local radio station, Radio Ngati Porou.

Jack Pokai and Ned Te Raunu were in their own words 'pretty stoked' when their team won the 1999 NPC Third Division final. They also won the 'Best Banner' competition and a cheque for $500.

ABOVE: The Te Araroa rugby sports domain and clubrooms show the benefits of sponsorship.

RIGHT: Neat and tidy – the main stand of the Tokomaru rugby ground.

BELOW RIGHT: For most of the week, this paddock near Lottin Point supports cattle but come the odd weekend in winter, it is transformed into a rugby battleground.

ABOVE: The difference one game makes – the broadcast box going up at the Ruatoria main stand soon after the local team won the NPC Third Division title.

ABOVE: A common sight throughout the Coast – a playing field doubling as a grazing paddock. In this case it's a horse doing the honours on Ruatoria's rugby domain.

BELOW: The Kawakawa rugby scrum machine, Te Araroa. This model is fairly typical in rural districts where the brakes are applied with concrete or, as happens here, water-filled 44-gallon drums.

## Power packs

The 'Heath Robinson' approach to the local scrum machines would suggest that rugby on the Coast favours lineouts more than scrums. The concrete roller job, however, worked wonders for the 1999 East Coast reps.

# Can you believe it?

PRIOR TO THE START of the 1999 representative season, the 'smart money' was not placed on East Coast winning the third division title. Some had billed it the Battle of the Titans, and most Bay supporters clearly believed their team would win. Although the East Coast team had worked its way solidly up the ladder during the season, few Bay supporters believed that the East Coast team would prevail.

But those Bay supporters hadn't reckoned on the character of the East Coast team or on the prowess of its coach, Joe McClutchie. Joe had instilled in them a no-nonsense approach to the basic requirements of the game and when the opening whistle blew on 15 October 1999, they were primed to the hilt.

Nearly 5000 people watched the game that day in Ruatoria – a huge turnout considering the population of the East Coast is approximately 6500. Among the more vocal local supporters was Bremner Mills who has followed the team's progress in virtually every game since the early 1980s.

For most of the game it was a neck-and-neck struggle but the final result was sealed by an inspired drop kick from Third Division Player of the Year and star of the match, Victor Taingahue. And when the final whistle blew the 18–15 result (in East Coast's favour) said it all.

Flags, banners, wigs and painted faces
ensured plenty of noise and support
from the East Coast fans. The die
was cast and the battle began
between the Scarlet Reds from
Poverty Bay and the proud Ngati Porou
East Coasters in sky blue.

'When the final whistle blew, you would
have thought we had won the World Cup!'

Bremner Mill

Warming the troops – Ngati Porou style

# EAST COAST

**15. DOONE HARRISON**
Kiwi Tea rooms

**14. JASON BRIGHT/MAIKA VERE**
Ngati Porou Whanui Forest/Pat Blinkhorne Forestry Ltd

**11. KORO NGARIMU**
Hikurangi Foodmarket

**13. TYRONE DELAMERE**
Te Araroa Hotel

**12. SETARIKI KAUNICARAMAKI**
Pat Blinkhorne Forestry Ltd

EAST-COAST-RUGBY UNION

**10. VICTOR TAINGAHUE**
Hikurangi Holdings

**9. JOHN NUKUNUKU**
Waiapu Work Trust

**8. WIRIHANA RAIHANIA (C)**
Te Runanga O Ngati Porou

**7. HORACE LEWIS**
Wrightsons

**6. TOKA LIKU**
Kai Kart Ruatoria

**5. KELE LEAWERE**
Bill Burdett

**4. INIA ROKO**
Pat Blinkhorne Forestry Ltd

**3. QUENTIN CARMICHAEL**
Ian Smith Transport

**2. DEREK LEEFE**
Williams & Kettle

**1. SAM MATENGA**
Eastern Buses

Reserves: 16. Ben Reedy (Transport & Marine Ruatoria) 17. Arthur Green (K & M Contractors) 18.Graeme Walker (Colbert Buses) 19. Bailey Mackey (Radio Ngati Porou) 20. Morgan Waitoa (Te Araroa Autos) 21. Huki Wilson (Prince Ferris) 22. Marijan Manuel (DTR). William Manuel (Ruatoria United Sports Club) Vere/Bright  Tyrone Mauheni (Hayden Partnership). Coach: Joe McClutchie (Horouta Sports Club). Assistent manager: Eli Manuel Waiapu Hotel). Manager: Anthony Nelson (Horouta Sports Club) Physiotherapist: Roger Main (G Hennah & G Kaiwai) Masseur: Jum Reedy (Morris Mataira).

**ABOVE:** The official programme for the final showing the level of support for the East Coast team with local companies sponsoring individual players.

**LEFT:** Sideline cheerleaders – East Coast style.

**RIGHT:** Kele Leawere dishing up some quality ball for the back-line troops.

# The Star of the Show!

**ABOVE & ABOVE RIGHT:** The star of the show, Victor Taingahue showing some of the dazzling form that earned him the title of Third Division Player of the Year.

**RIGHT:** Victor clinching the game with the game-breaking winning drop-kick.

**ABOVE**: Post-match victory haka – the intense pride of the team after winning the match.

**LEFT**: Skipper Wirihana Raihania triumphantly accepting the 1999 Air New Zealand Third Division Trophy.

**BELOW LEFT**: Joe McClutchie modestly acknowledging winning the trophy for the 1999 Rugby Coach of the Year.

**RIGHT**: A moment in history – the scoreboard confirms the final result.

No prouder moment for East Coast rugby –
winners of the 1999 NPC Third Division final

# Foreword

I WAS BORN and bred in Greymouth and I've lived here all my life so I feel that I qualify as a true blue 'West Coaster'. The West Coast has been good to me providing education and employment, and I have run my own business here for the past twenty-seven years. I still have friends from primary school, and in my teens and early twenties other friendships developed that are still very strong today. I met many friends through yachting and rugby – but it is the fellowship of rugby that I treasure the most.

The West Coast is probably the way it is because it lacks a big population; almost everybody knows everyone! I can travel anywhere on the Coast and run into someone to have a talk or a beer with.

During my time on the NZRFU, I travelled frequently by car to and from Christchurch, taking air connections to other destinations. On the return journey, whenever I reached the top of the Otira Gorge, I always felt I was home. I could smell the fresh air, the trees, the rain.

The friendliness, the sincerity of the people and their honesty, make me proud to be a Coaster.

And finally if I had one piece of sound advice for the NZRFU – retain the third division and continue to foster the game in New Zealand at the grass-roots level.

Ron Messenger
*Greymouth 2000*

# Golden days

RUGBY ON THE West Coast goes back to the very origins of the game in New Zealand. The Westport Club began life in 1892, the same year that the New Zealand Rugby Football Union was founded. The following year a tournament was held at Westport which featured teams from the Westport club, Cape Foulwind, Reefton and Greymouth. A few years later, in 1895, the Buller Union kicked off.

In those days, the West Coast supported large mining industries, and the hard men from the coal-mining towns of Denniston and Granity soon emerged as the king pins of the club scene at the turn of the century. Then, as today, isolation was a problem for those living on the Coast. An away game against Canterbury,

for example, was a three-day affair – a 20-hour journey each way from Greymouth on the stagecoach.

Over the years the West Coast-Buller region has produced 14 All Blacks, including Kenneth Svenson and Jack Steel who were both part of the 1924–25 Invincibles tour of the British Isles.

Today the two West Coast unions span a vast area. The Buller region stretches from midway between Westport and Greymouth, through to Karamea in the north and eastwards towards Reefton and Murchison. The West Coast union mainly embraces the regions that surround the towns of Greymouth and Hokitika and the sub-union of South Westland, which covers the area between Ross and Whataroa.

Unfortunately, many of the problems that afflict the East Coast also afflict these two unions. Ron Messenger, former president of the NZRFU and one of the Coast's staunchest supporters, believes the problem stems from isolation, a lack of work opportunity, and our current national preoccupation with the NPC First Division and the Super 12s.

Yet Ron also believes that they're a tough, individualistic breed on the Coast. He sees rugby still being played there for many years to come at representative and club level. And so it will as long as there are great men of rugby who continue to run and promote the game with passion and loyalty.

## The way it was

'In the first spell the ball was kicked over the fence behind the goal posts by one of the Brunner boys; another of them, jumping over, touched down and claimed a try. The try was allowed by the referee.'

*Grey River Argus*, September 9, 1889

**ABOVE**: The first Buller team – 1895.

**LEFT**: In the 1890s, the stagecoach and train trip from Greymouth to Christchurch took 20 hours.

## Buller Union All Blacks

Samuel Bligh (1910)

Thomas Fisher (1914)

Charles McLean (1920)

Kenneth 'Snowy' Svenson (1922, 1924–5)

Robert Tunnicliff (1923)

Edward Holder (1932, 1934)

William (Bill) Mumm, jnr (1949)

## West Coast Union All Blacks

Henry Butland (1893–94)

John Corbett (1905)

Henry Atkinson (1913)

Frank Freitas (1928)

Ron King (1934–38)

Graham (Mike) Gilbert (1935–36)

Jack Steel (1920–25)

ABOVE: In the early 1900s Denniston was New Zealand's leading coalfield, and home to some 1500 residents. This shot from 1924 depicts the seniors awaiting kick-off on their gravel and sand playing field. Depending on the opponents available, they alternated between union and league.

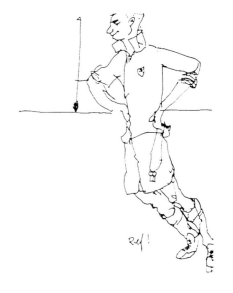

# The 1956 Rugby strike

It's not often that a provincial team is thrust into the national limelight. But that's what happened during the 1956 Springbok tour when a combined West Coast-Buller team went on strike – the only representative team ever to do so. The trouble started as they were preparing to play the Springboks mid-week.

All the Buller squad members had played club rugby on the previous Saturday, and then they were instructed by the Buller Union to play an additional town-and-country fixture to pick the team for the Seddon Shield Challenge the following Saturday. That left them playing four games in one week – a ridiculous situation, especially so when an international fixture was involved.

So they went on strike, holding their ground in the changing rooms and refusing to play a Sunday trial until some rugby administrative sanity prevailed. It took a few hours of delicate negotiating, but just prior to the 3 pm kick-off the game was officially cancelled.

Their stance earned them considerable national publicity at the time and a lot of support. And although they lost their mid-week match against the Springboks 27–6, the Buller boys won the Seddon Shield from Nelson 14–6 the following Saturday.

# Arthur Stanley Fong (MBE)

Arthur Fong's record as a New Zealand referee is truly remarkable – he spent 50 years refereeing the game, and was still doing 80 minutes at the age of 73.

Before then he represented the Coast for seven seasons as a member of the Star Club in Greymouth and represented the South Island as a five-eighth in 1933. However, international recognition was to come from another quarter in 1939 when he decided to become a referee.

From 1945 to 1956, Arthur controlled 26 international and representative fixtures including two test matches – the All Blacks' first test against Australia in 1946 and the third test against the British Isles in 1950.

The most notable aspect of his refereeing style was that he played the game principally for the enjoyment of the players. He played the advantage rule to the max – so much so that during the Kiwis v. Canterbury fixture in 1946, he didn't set the first scrum until 23 minutes had elapsed.

On the Coast, he became regarded as something of a legend, a higher authority to which all disputes involving rugby would be referred. His son Graeme recalls how the phone would often ring in the middle of the night, usually on a Saturday, from someone in a bar somewhere in New Zealand wanting to settle a disagreement as to who scored what try, where and whenever!

Arthur died in 1999 at the age of 93.

ABOVE: Arthur Fong awarding an All Black try in the first test against Australia in 1946 – his first test appointment.

LEFT: Arthur Fong – born to lead – West Coast representatives, 1933.

**ABOVE**: Fullback Rodney Dawes kicking for touch before a concerted Taranaki charge during Buller's unsuccessful 1964 challenge for the Ranfurly Shield. Taranaki won 11–0.

**LEFT**: State of Origin – the annual scrap between Buller and West Coast.

**AVOVE RIGHT**: Buller winger Brian Stack scores against West Coast, Westport, 1968. Stack had tremendous pace and should have been an All Black but placed family ahead of the silver fern when playing at his peak during the late 60s.

RIGHT: True blue Coast club rugby –
beards, socks around the ankles, plenty
of sticking plaster and tape, and a good
old-fashioned line-out struggle to claim
the ball.

BELOW: Buller's 1953 Ranfurly Shield
challenge at Lancaster Park. Ross
Smith is being tackled by Max (Barney)
White. Second five-eighth Tom Hawes is
the Buller player in support.

FOLLOWING PAGES: The South Westland
Seniors clearly illustrating what it feels
like to win the 1996 Senior Club
championships on the West Coast.

# Fair dinkum blokes

## Ron Messenger

Talk rugby on the West Coast and the name Ron Messenger invariably crops up. He is one of rugby's most passionate supporters, and much of his life has been dedicated to the 'nuts and bolts' administration of the game. Ron began his career playing club rugby for Blaketown during the 1950s. For 20 years he served on the West Coast RFU and in 1976 was elected president of the NZRFU. It was during his time on the NZRFU that Ron helped push through changes that resulted in the creation of the Third Division.

Ron's commitment to the game also stems from his deep love of the Coast. Born and bred in Greymouth, he has lived there all his life and feels qualified to call himself a 'true blue West Coaster'. The West Coast has been good to him – it educated him and then employed him, and for the last 27 years has enabled him to run his own business. He likes the fact that he can travel anywhere on the Coast and always run into someone to have a chat or a beer with. And although his time on the NZRFU has often taken him to other parts of the country, he never feels at home until once more he has travelled through the Otira Gorge and can smell the fresh air, the trees and the rain of his beloved West Coast.

For him, his long service to the game has simply been his special way of repaying his debt to his community.

## John Sturgeon

John was All Black manager from 1988 to 1991. This coincided with a very successful era for All Black rugby when Alex Wylie was coach. Before then he was on the West Coast Union management committee for 10 years from 1976 to 1986. He is also a life member of the Star United Club in Greymouth and the West Coast Union.

As an administrator, he has always placed a strong focus on the prime ingredient of the game – the players. In this he is like Ron Messenger, and holds strong views as to why so many talented Buller and West Coast players seek the richer rugby rewards on offer from the main centres. He has seen the strength of club rugby in the region decline over the past 20 years, while at a national level the game has become increasingly modelled on corporate lines. He believes modern rugby is now largely geared to an elitist group of about 200 players who reside in the main centres and play rugby there.

John's ability as a leading rugby administrator was clearly illustrated early this year when he enticed the Auckland Blues across from Christchurch for a training camp and rugby tuition for the youngsters on the Coast.

To see their idols in person and receive rugby instruction in their neck of the woods was a rugby blessing for the Coast's youth. The Crusaders and Highlanders also travel to the Coast, and such pilgrimages are vital for maintaining a strong interest in the game within the schools and the clubs of small unions like the Buller and West Coast.

## John 'Twinkle Toes' Hunt

A grass-roots rugby enthusiast from the top drawer, John (below left) has been there and done that in the very best traditions of a true Coaster.

He earned his rugby 'purple patch' in 1953 as first five-eighth of a very talented Buller team. That same year he was also an All Black trialist – this was when the rules gave players from the smaller unions a chance of a look-in at becoming an All Black.

One of his most vivid memories occurred in 1956 when the Buller reps went on strike during a series of altercations with the hierarchy over too many fixtures within a very restricted time-frame.

During his coaching days in the 1960s and 70s, John had few equals on the Coast, and was highly regarded not only for his coaching skills but also for his overall knowledge of the game.

Now in semi-retirement, John occupies much of his spare time honing his art skills on the easel, and in the rugby season giving his utmost support to both Buller and the West Coast.

**BELOW**: John 'Twinkle Toes' Hunt heading for the try-line with four Canerbury players in pursuit during a Ranfurly Shield Challenge. The Buller first five-eighth had broken his nose in a regional All Black trial a few weeks before. Also featured in this shot are five players who were, or would become, All Blacks – Ross Smith, Doug Wilson, Kevin Stuart, Pat Vincent and Bill Mumm. Canterbury won the game 19–6.

## A Buller 'Tough Nut'

One of the great characters of Buller is a prop who traded under the name of 'Juicy Joe' Syron. He started his Buller rep days (1961–73) as a No. 8, and ended them as a no-nonsense prop. Andy Haden and Alistair Hopkinson were two of the more notable 'big shots' who under-estimated the mean side of 'Juicy Joe' and, as a result, both came off second best. Somewhere in between rugby and farming, he also staked a claim to and won an Australian light heavy-weight boxing title.

Juicy now lives at Waimangaroa on the road towards Karamea and milks a herd of 250 cows.

# Heart of the coast

To EVEN THE most casual observer it is apparent that rugby is part of the life-blood of the Coast. It is part of their identity. Most small towns have their clubrooms, and goal posts are a familiar sight from the road. Go into any pub and the conversation will turn to rugby, and there you will meet characters bigger than life. On the Coast, local rugby legends are respected in a way not found in the cities.

Like most small unions in New Zealand, the Buller and West Coast unions have access to a strong pool of players at the junior level. But once kids leave college, work opportunities are often quite limited. So to keep numbers up at club level, both unions have solved the problem by amalgamating players and teams under one club banner.

Buller has currently only three senior club sides playing in the senior competition; West Coast has four. And although times are tough, you won't find many complaints.

LEFT: Tom Green – true blue Coaster and local identity. He loves his rugby but not as much as he does the public bar of the Little Wanganui Hotel near Karamea.

RIGHT: Thomas Stewart, the current Buller No. 8 and the NPC's leading player for the most games (160) for his union. Thomas began his record-breaking trot as a 17-year-old in 1984, and one more game will see him pass Alan Sutherland's Nelson-Marlborough record of 137 games on the trot. (Thomas is injured and he currently shares the record with Sutherland – Ed)

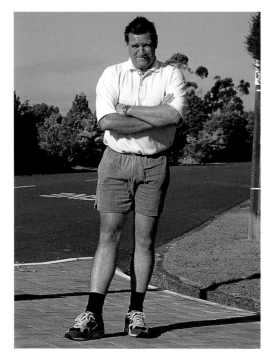

**ABOVE LEFT**: Evan Fox – a long-serving Buller referee since 1985, with 52 first-class games under his belt, having a pit-stop while doing the hard yards with some pre-season road training.

**ABOVE RIGHT**: Ref Alistair Smith cleaning his whistle via the courtesy of Alex Gibson's water bucket!

**LEFT**: Two of the Coast's zambucks. True stalwarts – where would we be without them— Garry Adamson and Charlie Blanchett.

ABOVE: Karamea rugby headquarters – the public bar of the Little Wanganui Hotel.

RIGHT: The legendary Jim Blair giving treatment and instruction on how best to avoid injury for the 'boys' on the Coast.

## Those 'good old days'

'The Reefton Football Club will play their first match of the season today. The match is to be played in the interval between the races (the Reefton Racing Club's) and will start at 2 p.m.'

*Inangahua Herald*, Reefton, April 10, 1896

**ABOVE**: The caretakers of the Karamea Rugby Domain, Jocelyn and Bob Colville, sitting down to a midday 'nosh' at the Do Duck Inn, Westport.

**LEFT**: The 'golden oldies' of Collingwood – Don McKnight, Tinky Hovenden and Selwyn Tasker. By the look of them, a pre-season course with Jenny Craig wouldn't be out of the question. Tinky is the proprietor of the Collingwood Hotel and still believes that he was desperately unlucky not to be called up for duty for the 1960 tour of South Africa.

**RIGHT**: Myrtle and Melvin, owners of the Karamea Motel. Melvin displays similar traits to 'One Game Henry' from Waverley – he can't be bothered with all that modern 'show pony' nonsense and much prefers to look after 'Mum' – and ride his old 2-wheeler bike instead!

**ABOVE**: Westport support crew – behind the rope, early season 2000.

**LEFT**: Hokitika Kiwi club stalwarts Wayne Stuart and Bill Jones – true to the cause in their love and support of the game in their local region.

**RIGHT**: Half-time running repairs – Buller style!

The great leveller — playing rugby in the winter mud and rain. And few like it better than the boys from Buller and the West Coast.

TOP: Rugby Park, Greymouth.

LEFT: Cass Square, Hokitika.

**ABOVE & LEFT**: The No. 1 stand of the Greymouth Rugby Park – arguably one of New Zealand's finest rugby grounds. In the 1999 season, 86 games were played on it and hardly a blade of grass was disturbed.

**OPPOSITE, ABOVE RIGHT**: A common sight in grass-roots rugby with a local hotel and brewery sponsoring the home team – the Blaketown Club, Greymouth. A transport company does likewise in Murchison.

**OPPOSITE, BELOW RIGHT**: Kumara Sports Domain may not be attracting the crowds of old but the grand-stand proudly demonstrates the richness of the game of rugby in the rural grass-roots of New Zealand.

**ABOVE & LEFT**: Hokitika's Wests Club raising funds by opening its doors and offering a bed and breakfast for transit visitors to Hokitika's annual Wild Foods Festival.

LEFT: A West Coast original – and Houhou Timbers owns a beauty!

BELOW: Gary Schroder and the boys from the Kiwi and Wests Clubs helping to raise funds in the big beer tent, Wild Foods Festival.

ABOVE: Bob and Jocelyn Colville are the caretakers of the Karamea Sports Domain. They live six months of the year in a big mobile rig parked alongside the washing line-cum-grandstand with Barnie, a 24-year-old parrot.

RIGHT: Hannes, Kris and Percy from South Africa had a lifetime experience during their month-long rugby tour in New Zealand. Half of the town turned up for their fixture with Westport College.

RIGHT: The Grey Valley Rugby Club score-board facility at Pendy Park, Ikamatua.

BELOW: The Westport Trotting Club. Many small towns in rural New Zealand share costs by maintaining joint rugby and racetrack facilities.

ABOVE: Club stalwart Noeline and her granddaughter Tiana on guard duty outside the Kiwi clubrooms in Hokitika – Wild Foods weekend.

OPPOSITE, ABOVE: Kay Pearson giving the big heave-ho with the post-match wash for Hokitika's Wests rugby jerseys.

OPPOSITE, RIGHT: Tracey Kearns doing the honours with the weekly jersey wash for the Hokitika Kiwi seniors. Tracey coaches the Kiwi under 9s and her grandfather, grandmother and her dad, Andy, are all life members of the club.

OPPOSITE, FAR RIGHT: Gerald Hart was a fullback for West Coast-Buller and kicked four penalties when they defeated Australia 15–10 in 1972. Gerald and his wife Janine have eight children – four boys and four girls. Three of the boys, Wayne, Richard and Michael followed in dad's footsteps but youngest boy Brett, according to mum, showed little interest in the game.

# More of the 'little fellas'

**ABOVE LEFT**: Local 'little fellas' – Samuel, Craig, Ben and Jack – at Otira Domain near Arthur's Pass. The domain is down to one set of posts and a field badly in need of a good cut.

**ABOVE**: Twelve-year-old Jordan and Andrew honing their rugby skills in what may well be New Zealand's smallest rugby field and posts – the Curtain's backyard, Ruatapu.

**LEFT**: Youngsters from Blackball Primary School, which has a roll of 52.

**OPPOSITE, RIGHT**: If the headmaster of Kumara Primary School had his way, his pupils would be digging for gold. The 'good oil' says that the field sits on top of rich gold reserves.

**OPPOSITE, ABOVE LEFT**: Pre-season and no posts on show for a few of the kids from Granity District School – the school roll is 140.

**OPPOSITE, LEFT**: The pupils of Inangahua School plus Dolly the Labrador in the front of the rugby posts of their recently refurbished 50m field. The school's roll stands at 13.

**ABOVE**: The Westport under 17s toughing it out with some tackle bag practice at the Westport Rugby Grounds.

**RIGHT**: Westport fullback Tim Manawatu, an 18-year-old rising star with a bright future.

# The Ross Connection

When rugby families of past generations are being discussed, such names as Going, Clarke and Meads come readily to mind.

Situated 40 kilometres south of Hokitika is the small South Westland township of Ross – and home base for another highly respected rugby family, the Foster tribe!

Kevin Foster (senior) was the eldest of 12 children – six boys and six girls. In turn, he and his wife Margaret have raised a family of four boys and a daughter.

Kevin (senior) represented West Coast for 7 seasons from 1953 to 1960. The four boys – David, Kevin, Terry, and Michael – have all appeared for the West Coast during the past 20 years.

The eldest son David started refereeing after his playing days were over and is currently ranked No. 1 NPC divisional referee on the Coast. Michael is currently captain of the West Coast team, and since his 'eye-opener' outing which Canterbury won 128–0, he has notched up 81 appearances for the Coast.

**ABOVE**: Dad and the boys at the Woodham Shield Challenge, Fox Glacier, in 1991. That day all the boys took to the field in the same team. From left: Kevin, Michael, David, Kevin (senior), and Terry.

**OPPOSITE, RIGHT**: Dave, Kevin and Peter of the Foster clan sharing a jug outside the Empire Hotel, Ross.

**ABOVE LEFT**: Eleven-year-old Eve Helly, seen here on the new Ross rugby field, plays rugby during the week at St Patrick's School in Greymouth.

**ABOVE RIGHT**: Grass-roots rugby at its very best. Eight-year-old Matt Costello, seen here in front of his Ross Primary School posts, plays for the South Westland midgets. For the small fee of $10, jerseys and boots are provided from a pool for all juniors who participate in the game in this region. His father John also informed me that many of the kids from this neck of the woods make a 3–4 hour bus trip each way to play a set of round-robin 20-minute games in Greymouth. The highlight – when the bus stops at 'Porkies' in Hokitika for the compulsory return-trip feed of fish & chips!

ABOVE: Ross also lays claim to owning the biggest 'footy' roller on show in the country!

BELOW: The Ross rugby field that was opposite the pub and most surely the richest provincial rugby field in New Zealand. The Birchfield Mining Company has borrowed it for a while, but it's coming back once the gold reserves have dried up.

# The rugby girls

WHERE WOULD THE game of rugby be without them?

They cook, they iron and they wash – and mostly just for the love of the game. Since the beginnings of the game on the West Coast, the ladies' committees have been an indispensable part of club life – part of the glue that holds the local community together.

And if that's not enough, these days they'll often be seen on Saturday as either a coach or a referee. In the junior grades it's now a common sight to see the girls on the same footing as that of the boys – a sign of the times.

## West Coast tucker

### Auntie Kay's Aftermatch Pie

Flaky pastry
1kg sausage meat
2 tbsp sauce or relish
1 beaten egg
Salt and pepper
1 large finely chopped onion
½ cup soft breadcrumbs
1 grated apple
Optional: Left-over carrots, peas or frozen mixed vegetables

■ Line a large sponge roll dish with flaky pastry. Mix the above ingredients together and spread over pastry. Cover top with cut tomato slices and sprinkle with oregano and basil. Bake in a moderate oven for approximately 45 minutes. Serve as hot or cold slices.

*Thanks to Kay from Hokitika*

ABOVE: The Denniston Community Miners' Hall – the post-match venue for the early nineteenth-century rugby fixtures that were played on the gravel-and-sand field situated nearby.

RIGHT: Spoiling their men rotten – the 1956 Kiwi Club Ladies' Committee, Hokitika.

BELOW: What she lacks in brawn she makes up for in speed. Wendy Clark going for the gap in a Sunday Golden Oldies fixture on the Coast.

### Kev's Favourite Whitebait Pie

Flaky pastry
500g whitebait
3 eggs
Pinch of salt and pepper
Mixed vegetables of your choice

■ Roll out flaky pastry and line an ovenproof dish. Mix the ingredients together and place in dish. Cover with pastry. Bake for 1 hour or until cooked in a moderate oven. Ideal cold and great for lunches.

*Thanks to Margaret Foster from Ross*

### Granny Eckersley's Shortbread

225g butter
3 tbsp icing sugar
3 tbsp cornflour
225g flour
Pinch of salt

■ Cream the butter and icing sugar together, add the remaining ingredients and form into a roll. Cut off slices and place on a cold tray to be baked 20 minutes in a moderate oven.

*Thanks to Granny Exckersley from Denniston*

OPPOSITE: The Buller Café. Their speciality – fish & chips and whitebait fritters.

ABOVE: The Miners' Hall, Runanga. The banner says it all – 'United we stand. Divided we fall.'

RIGHT: Murtle and the girls from the Christchurch Old Boys' Football Club having a bit of pre-season fun at the Big Day Out in Hokitika.

OVERLEAF: The main street, Westport.

'At the last game the opposition complained about the shocking state of the pitch. So this week members were engaged on Saturday grubbing the rushes off the Recreation Ground.'

*Grey River Argus*, May 17, 1886

'Whenever the ball became loose the order was given to "fall on it", a very unmanly thing and one likely to disgrace the noble game of football.'

*Grey River Argus*, May 25, 1886

# East meets west

The 1999 West Coast reps missed out on the final by a whisker, but not so for their synchronised 'Star Status' fan club who emerged as the third division market leaders.

ABOVE: West Coast favourites – the Kokatahi Band. No touring international rugby team has left the Coast without experiencing the magnificent sound and hospitality associated with this famous band.

LEFT: No doubt about this lad's loyalty.

BELOW: The local cheerleaders giving it their best shot in support of their West Coast heroes.

FOLLOWING PAGES: East meets West – Raynor Park, Westport 1999. The boys from East Coast Ngati Porou doing the business versus Buller during their march towards claiming the elusive third division title.

East meets West, Raynor Park, Westport

## Heartland West Coast

TOP: The Empire Hotel, Ross, South Westland.

BOTTOM: Morning 'smoko' for the boys at Houhou Timbers, near Hokitika.

## Match — East Coast and West Coast — 17 August 1996 — Ruatoria.

LEFT: East Coast blindside flanker has got hold of the ball, but for most of the game the East Coast boys found it difficult to pierce the West Coast defence.

LEFT: East Coast halfback Kahu Waitoa was firing out some good bullets all day, but the friendly foe from the West Coast ended up winning the game 24–10.

LEFT: Scrag-time for West Coast's teenage star Craig de Goldi, but four years down the track it's a much different story. Craig is now firmly established as one of the stars of the world-aclaimed New Zealand Sevens squad.

**ABOVE**: And closer to home, the annual third division battle between West Coast and Buller always features grass-roots rugby at its very best.

**OPPOSITE, ABOVE**: The 98 West Coast boys stripping from their No. 1's into tracksuits (on the Gisborne Airport tarmac) en route to Ruatoria.

**OPPOSITE, BELOW**: Four hours later it's warming up prior to a light training run (Ruatoria Domain) for the annual East Coast encounter – East Coast won 35–15.